Original title:
When I'm Brave

Copyright © 2024 Creative Arts Management OÜ
All rights reserved.

Author: Natalia Harrington
ISBN HARDBACK: 978-9916-88-964-0
ISBN PAPERBACK: 978-9916-88-965-7

Shadows Turned to Light

In the dark where whispers sigh,
Flickers dance and memories fly.
Hope ignites the blackest night,
Turning shadows into light.

A gentle hand, a guiding spark,
Illuminates the tender heart.
With every step, the fears take flight,
As shadows turn to purest light.

Leaps into Tomorrow

With courage wrapped in fragile dreams,
We rise above the silent themes.
Each leap a choice, a brand new way,
Into the dawn of a bright new day.

Through winding paths of the unknown,
We gather strength, no longer alone.
Hope carries us, our spirits high,
As we leap into the open sky.

Echoes of Boldness

In the stillness, a voice rings clear,
Whispers of courage we hold dear.
Bold steps taken, hearts aligned,
Echoes linger, unconfined.

Through valleys deep and mountains tall,
We find our path, we heed the call.
Each echo weaves a story bright,
Of battles fought and gained our sight.

Against the Current

Against the flow, we stand our ground,
In fierce currents, strength is found.
With steadfast hearts, we will not sway,
We chart our course, come what may.

The waters rush but we remain,
Through storms and trials, joy and pain.
With every stroke, we fight the tide,
Against the current, we won't hide.

Stepping Stones of Grit

Each stone we tread is rough and worn,
They bear the weight of dreams reborn.
We lift our feet, we move ahead,
Through every doubt, through every thread.

In shadows deep, our spirits rise,
With every march, we claim the skies.
The path may twist, the road may bend,
But on we go, we will not end.

A journey long, with heart in hand,
We carve our hopes upon this land.
Each step a mark of strength and will,
In grit we trust, our dreams to fulfill.

Together strong, we face the fire,
United still, we'll never tire.
These stepping stones, our battles fought,
With every leap, our courage sought.

The Dance of Defiance

In moonlit nights, we find our stance,
With fierce hearts, we dare to dance.
Each step a rebellion, bold and free,
    Against the tide, our spirits flee.

The rhythm pulses in our veins,
With every spin, we break the chains.
The world may scoff, but we will stand,
In defiance strong, we take command.

Our voices rise, a song unchained,
With passion fierce, we are unfeigned.
Through whispered doubts, we take our flight,
In every twirl, we claim our right.

So let them stare, let them conspire,
In unity, we grow higher.
This dance of defiance, wild and true,
In every heartbeat, we break through.

Heartbeats of the Dauntless

In the silence, we hear the call,
Echoes of courage in the hall.
Each heartbeat a step toward the light,
Fierce and steady, we join the fight.

With fearless hearts, the path we claim,
Through trials faced, we fan the flame.
Together we stand, through thick and thin,
In every struggle, our hearts begin.

The pulse of hope, it drives us near,
With dauntless spirit, we conquer fear.
Each heartbeat a drum, a steady beat,
In the face of doubt, we won't retreat.

With every breath, we rise anew,
Together we're strong, together true.
In heartbeats bold, our strength will soar,
As dauntless souls, we'll face the war.

Standing Tall Through the Storm

When winds may howl and shadows creep,
We stand our ground, our vows to keep.
Each raindrop falls as battles waged,
In unwavering strength, we're engaged.

The storm may roar, but we shall stand,
With hearts like steel, we take command.
Through fiercest trials, we won't bend,
Our spirits fierce, we will not end.

In torrents wild, we find our grace,
In every challenge, we find our place.
Together we shine, through darkest night,
With courage strong, we seek the light.

So let the storm come, and let it rage,
With every heartbeat, we turn the page.
In unity fierce, we'll rise above,
Through every tempest, we stand in love.

Freedom in the Leap

Above the clouds, I dare to rise,
With heavy chains, I sever ties.
The wind it whispers, soft and sweet,
In open skies, my heart's retreat.

With every heartbeat, courage comes,
I take a breath, and freedom hums.
Into the void, I cast my dream,
A life reborn, a brighter gleam.

I touch the stars, embrace the night,
My spirit soaring, pure delight.
In leaps I find, my soul's release,
A dance of joy, a song of peace.

Unfurling the Tapestry of Valor

Threads of courage intertwined,
A story woven, strong and kind.
Each knot a struggle, each weave a chance,
In trials faced, we learn to dance.

Colors bright, horizons wide,
Through darkest paths, we walk with pride.
In battles fought, our hearts ignite,
Unfurling dreams, we embrace the fight.

With every stitch, a lesson learned,
In unity, our passion burned.
Together stand, we weave the light,
A tapestry of hope in sight.

Feet Firmly Planted

With roots deep set in the earth,
My heart knows well its place of birth.
Through storms and trials, I shall not sway,
With feet firm planted, come what may.

The winds may howl, the skies may dark,
Yet in my soul, a steady spark.
I draw my strength from every grain,
A testament to joy and pain.

In stillness found, my spirit thrives,
A tranquil peace, where courage drives.
With feet so grounded, I will rise,
For strength is born where hope abides.

Navigating through Tempests

Waves crash high against the bow,
Steering through the howling storm.
The compass spins, yet I must vow,
To find my way, to stay warm.

Stars conceal behind dark clouds,
Lightning flashes, a fleeting guide.
Hope emerges from sea's loud shrouds,
As I navigate the swell with pride.

Each gust whispers a tale of fear,
Yet in my heart, a flame still glows.
With every challenge drawing near,
The sailor learns, resilience grows.

At dawn's break, the tempest fades,
The calm reveals a gentle tide.
Through trials faced and plans remade,
A hero's journey shall abide.

In the Silence of Courage

Whispers echo in quiet halls,
Where doubts linger and shadows play.
Yet deep within my spirit calls,
A voice that guides me through the fray.

In moments lost and paths unsure,
I find a strength, an inner fire.
In silence, courage does endure,
With resolve that never tires.

The heart beats strong against the hush,
Each pulse a testament to fight.
Through darkest times, I will not rush,
For in the calm, I find my light.

So let the world around me spin,
I stand my ground, I will not break.
In silence born, my peace begins,
With each small step, I dare to take.

The Heart's Uncharted Path

Footsteps tread on whispered dreams,
A trail unknown, yet calling near.
Beneath the stars, my spirit beams,
As shadows blend with every fear.

Each choice a wave, each turn a chance,
To dance with fate, embrace the thrill.
A journey woven by circumstance,
With every heartbeat, I'm fulfilled.

The wildflowers bow to my stride,
Their vibrant hues, a map in bloom.
With every step, I turn the tide,
As courage lifts the weight of gloom.

Through tangled woods and valleys low,
My heart uncovers paths anew.
In every sunset's fiery glow,
I chase horizons, bold and true.

Singing with the Wind

A gentle breeze begins to hum,
With secrets carried from afar.
It dances softly, beats like a drum,
As whispers mingle with the stars.

In harmony with leaves that sway,
Voices rise in joyful tune.
Nature's choir, night and day,
A song of love beneath the moon.

With every gust, my heart takes flight,
The air alive with dreams and hope.
Together we embrace the night,
In melody, we learn to cope.

As dawn breaks forth, the songs remain,
In rippling streams and mountain peaks.
To sing with wind, to heed its claim,
A language only nature speaks.

Braving the Depths of Silence

In the stillness, whispers fade,
Echoes of thoughts that once were made.
Hearts can dance through quiet fears,
Finding strength in hidden tears.

Amid the shadows, courage grows,
A gentle spark the spirit sows.
Through silence deep, the soul will weave,
A tapestry of hope to believe.

Beneath the surface, currents flow,
Guiding hearts where few dare go.
A solemn vow to brave the dark,
In silence, we ignite the spark.

As dawn unfolds, the darkness wanes,
In quietude, we break the chains.
Each breath a testament of grace,
In silence, we find our rightful place.

An Ember's Resolve

A flicker glows in the dead of night,
An ember's warmth, an inner light.
Through storms that rage and winds that howl,
A steady heart, a fierce resolve.

Amidst the ashes, fire takes root,
With every challenge, we find our truth.
In the chaos, we stay alive,
An ember's pulse, a will to thrive.

Through trials faced, we gather strength,
In moments brief, we go the length.
With grit and grace, we rise anew,
An ember's resolve, steadfast and true.

In shadows cast, we choose to stand,
With courage etched in every hand.
From small beginnings, bold hearts ignite,
An ember's glow, a beacon bright.

The Courageous Mosaic

Each shard reflects a piece of fate,
Colors blended, unique and great.
Together forming a vibrant whole,
A courageous mosaic, heart and soul.

Through broken paths, we journey far,
Embracing every battle scar.
In unity, our stories entwine,
A tapestry of strength divine.

Each piece a whisper, soft yet loud,
With every hue, we stand unbowed.
Collectively, our voices rise,
A courageous song beneath the skies.

With courage bold, we take our stand,
Painting life with heart and hand.
In the mosaic of our days,
We find the strength to learn and blaze.

Shadows Turned to Light

In whispers low, the shadows creep,
Harvesting dreams the heart must keep.
Yet deep within, a spark ignites,
Transforming darkness into sights.

Each moment passed, a chance to grow,
From silent struggles, courage flows.
In shadows cast, new visions breathe,
With every dawn, the light we weave.

Through valleys deep where fears reside,
We journey forth, hearts open wide.
Embracing change, we take our flight,
In shadows turned, we find our light.

With every step, we shed the night,
In brave acceptance, hearts ignite.
Together we rise, spirits bright,
In shadows turned, we claim our right.

Courageous Palms Against the Storm

In the wind's fierce howl they stand,
Roots deep in the shifting sand,
Leaves raised high to greet the fight,
Courage blooms in the darkest night.

Raindrops fall, a heavy toll,
Yet they sway, they bend, they roll,
Whispers of strength echo within,
Palm fronds dance, they will not bend.

With every gust, with every strain,
The storm may come, but they'll remain,
Defiant in their steadfast grace,
Embracing trials they must face.

Courageous palms against the storm,
In nature's fury, they transform,
Bearing witness to life's great force,
They stand united, hearts of course.

The Light of Unyielding Hearts

In darkest hours, a faint glow,
From the hearts that choose to sow,
Seeds of hope in barren lands,
With every act, their glow expands.

Unyielding spirits, shining bright,
Casting shadows into light,
Together they form a shining trail,
An unbreakable bond that will not fail.

Through storms of doubt and fears that rise,
They glimpse the truth beyond the lies,
With courage drawn from deep inside,
They face the world, arms open wide.

The light that flickers in their chest,
Guiding souls through every quest,
Unyielding hearts will not be dimmed,
In unity, their spirits brim.

Ascending Beyond Barriers

Through the shadows, they begin to climb,
Scaling heights, transcending time,
With every step, they break the mold,
Creating stories yet untold.

Boundaries whisper, but they ignore,
For within their hearts lies a core,
Of strength that shatters every chain,
In the struggle, there's much to gain.

Each summit reached is a new dawn,
With winds of change, they carry on,
Hand in hand, they lift as one,
To grasp the light, to face the sun.

Ascending higher, they touch the sky,
With dreams that leap, they learn to fly,
Beyond the barriers, they find their way,
In a world reborn with each new day.

The Heart's Tenacious Anthem

In every beat, a tale unfolds,
A rhythm written, brave and bold,
The heart knows paths where others stall,
With tenacity, it answers the call.

Through trials faced, through paths unknown,
It charts a course, despite the stone,
With every challenge, it sings anew,
An anthem strong, a bond so true.

Together we rise, together we fall,
In harmony's grasp, we hear the call,
The heart's fierce song, its melody pure,
In unity, our spirits endure.

Resilience echoes through every chord,
An anthem of strength, our hearts restored,
With courage as our guiding light,
We journey forth, embracing the fight.

Charting Unfamiliar Waters

In the depths of uncharted seas,
Waves rise high, as hopes tease.
Stars above guide my way,
As night swallows the day.

With sails unfurled, I venture forth,
To find the treasures of the earth.
Strong winds whisper tales untold,
Of ancient lands and hearts of gold.

The compass spins, yet I press on,
Through storm and shadow until the dawn.
Each wave a lesson, each gust a guide,
In these waters, I confide.

Emerging from tempest, I see the light,
A shore appears, pure and bright.
Here begins a new chapter's start,
With fearless courage in my heart.

Embracing the Unseen

In the silence, whispers call,
Embracing shadows, I feel small.
Yet in the stillness, strength grows wide,
A gentle force, my faithful guide.

I tread the paths that few have known,
In hidden realms, I've often grown.
With open arms, I take the leap,
Into the depths where secrets sleep.

The veil is thin, the air is charged,
With echoes of dreams, so enlarged.
I chase the visions, bright and clear,
For in the unseen, there's nothing to fear.

Each moment unfolds, a sacred space,
Where shadows dance with tender grace.
I learn to trust what lies within,
Embracing the unseen, I begin.

The Journey of a Fearless Soul

Through valleys deep and mountains high,
The fearless soul will never shy.
With every step, a story told,
In sunlight's warmth or bitter cold.

On winding paths where few have trod,
A heart ablaze, a fervent nod.
For every trial, a lesson steep,
In endless dreams, their spirit leaps.

With courage forged in fire and strife,
They navigate the dance of life.
A traveler's heart, a restless mind,
In this journey, true gems find.

The horizon calls, a siren's song,
Where right feels right and wrong feels wrong.
With fearless resolve, they forge ahead,
In a world of marvels, proudly led.

A Song for the Unafraid

In shadows long, a brave heart sings,
Of hope that blooms on fragile wings.
With voices strong, together they rise,
To touch the clouds and pierce the skies.

Each note a beacon, bright and clear,
A melody that conquers fear.
The unafraid, with spirits bold,
Weave tales of love, adventures untold.

Through storms that howl and rivers wide,
They dance with joy, walk side by side.
In harmony, their souls unite,
Creating futures where all feels right.

So let them sing, let them be free,
With every breath, their legacy.
For in their voices, fierce and grand,
Lies strength to dream and take a stand.

Heartfelt Havoc

In the depths of love's embrace,
Passion blazes, leaves a trace.
Whispers soft, but thunder loud,
Hearts collide in a vibrant crowd.

Tears and laughter intertwine,
Moments fleeting, yet divine.
Storms may rage, but so do we,
In chaos, love will find its key.

Echoes dance in shadows cast,
Lessons learned, good times surpassed.
Every heartbeat, every sigh,
Crafts a story, never shy.

Through the wreckage, we emerge,
Stronger than we ever were.
Heartfelt havoc lays the ground,
For love's true beauty to be found.

In the Shadow of Giants

Beneath the reach of towering forms,
We tread softly, weathering storms.
Their voices whisper in the breeze,
Lessons hidden among the trees.

Paths of strength, we learn to walk,
In quiet moments, courage talks.
Every shadow holds a light,
Guiding us through the darkest night.

With every height, a depth we find,
The giants shape both heart and mind.
In their shade, we grow and thrive,
Finding grace to truly strive.

To stand tall, despite the fear,
Embrace the wisdom that is near.
In the shadow, we learn to soar,
And echo tales of giants yore.

Brave Footsteps in Sand

With every step upon the shore,
A tale unfolds, forevermore.
Footprints mark the path we take,
Bravery thrives with each heartache.

Waves crash hard, yet I stand tall,
Facing the tide, answering the call.
In the distance, horizons gleam,
Chasing hopes that dare to dream.

As the sun dips into the sea,
Every heartbeat sings to me.
The sand, a canvas of my plight,
Crafting moments, pure and bright.

In this journey, I find my way,
Through storms that darken every day.
Brave footsteps in sand remind,
That courage dwells within the mind.

The Silence Before the Roar

In the quiet, tension swells,
Mysteries hidden, secrets tell.
Nature pauses, breath held tight,
Awaiting the dawn, embracing light.

The heartbeats echo in the night,
Anticipation sparks the flight.
A stillness wrapped in soft embrace,
Hints of thunder, time to race.

Voices whisper, winds conspire,
Igniting a latent, burning fire.
In this lull, dreams take flight,
As shadows mingle with the light.

Then comes the roar, bold and clear,
The world awakens, shedding fear.
From silence birthed, the sound does soar,
Reminds us all what life is for.

A Leap into the Infinite

The sky is vast and wide,
Where dreams begin to soar,
With each step towards the edge,
Whispers call for more.

A heartbeat quickens now,
As doubts begin to fade,
In the silence before flight,
The soul is unafraid.

Above the clouds I rise,
Embracing endless blue,
With open arms I leap,
To find the world anew.

Wings spread in boundless grace,
I dance among the stars,
For in this leap of faith,
I'm free from earthly bars.

Courage in the Face of Fear

In shadows deep and dark,
Where doubts begin to grow,
A whisper of the heart,
Reminds me to be bold.

A tremor in my hands,
Yet still I stand my ground,
For courage lives within,
Where strength can be found.

With every step I take,
The echoes start to fade,
For fear is but a shadow,
In the light, I am brave.

Embracing what is true,
I walk this path alone,
For courage leads the way,
To places yet unknown.

A Heart Untamed

A wild heart breaks the cage,
With freedom as its song,
It dances in the moonlight,
Where wild spirits belong.

Untamed and ever bold,
It seeks the thrill of life,
With every beat it longs,
To rise above the strife.

In fields of golden dreams,
It runs with pure delight,
For chains cannot confine,
What yearns for endless flight.

A heart that knows no bounds,
Will always find a way,
To chase the stars above,
And greet the break of day.

Steps Toward the Sun

With each step I ascend,
Toward the golden glow,
The warmth upon my face,
Is where I long to go.

The path is winding slow,
Yet hope fuels every stride,
Each moment feels like flight,
With love as my guide.

The sunbeams pierce the haze,
Illuminating dreams,
In this journey of mine,
I hear the future's screams.

So forward I will go,
Embracing light and fun,
For every step I take,
Is one step toward the sun.

Walking through the Flames

Step by step, within the fire,
Courage stirs, hearts never tire.
Through the heat, we find our way,
Chasing shadows, come what may.

Embers flicker, courage bold,
Lessons learned, and stories told.
In the blaze, we shed our fears,
Rising stronger through the years.

Every spark ignites a dream,
Hope rekindled in the gleam.
Walking forward, hand in hand,
Together strong, together stand.

From the ashes, life will bloom,
In the dark, we find the room.
Walking through the flames of fate,
United still, we emulate.

Tides of Strength

Waves crash hard upon the shore,
With each rise, we learn to soar.
Tides that pull, tides that push,
In their strength, we feel the rush.

Underneath the vast expanse,
Life's currents lead us in a dance.
Every ebb holds lessons clear,
In the silent waves, we steer.

Though the storms may roar and swell,
Inside our hearts, we know it well.
Tides of strength, relentless call,
Together we shall never fall.

As the moon embraces night,
Guiding us with silver light.
Tides of strength, we find our way,
In their arms, we choose to stay.

The Pulse of Brave New Worlds

In the stillness, hear the beat,
Tales of courage, bold and sweet.
Each heart pounding, echoes loud,
In the crowd, we feel so proud.

Brave new worlds await our glance,
In the chaos, find our chance.
Every dream holds sacred space,
In the pulse, we find our grace.

Hands together, futures speak,
In our journey, not so bleak.
Feel the rhythm, come alive,
In our hearts, the dreams will thrive.

With each step, we carve the way,
A brave new world is here to stay.
The pulse runs deep, a guiding force,
Together we shall chart our course.

A Canvas of Wylde Colors

Brushstrokes wild, colors collide,
In this canvas, dreams abide.
Every hue a voice unique,
In the chaos, truth we seek.

Splashes bright, the heart's delight,
Painting stars against the night.
Vivid tales in strokes so bold,
In this canvas, life unfolds.

Every shade a story tells,
In the silence, magic dwells.
A dance of colors, hearts ignite,
Waltzing through the dark and light.

With each layer, we find our place,
In the art, we seek our grace.
A canvas of wylde colors bright,
Unleashing dreams, revealing light.

The Art of Vulnerable Valor

In silence, strength is born anew,
A heart laid bare, the courage grew.
With every scar, a tale unfolds,
The warmth of truth, the bravest gold.

To stand upright, though winds may blow,
In gentle grace, our spirits glow.
Embracing flaws, we find our way,
In tender strength, we choose to stay.

Conquering My Inner Giants

Battles fought within the mind,
A journey slow, yet so refined.
With every doubt, a whisper clear,
The giants fall when faced with fear.

I gather dreams, I weave them tight,
Each victory a surge of light.
The shadows tremble at my call,
In every rise, I choose to stand tall.

Fearless Threads Weaving Stories

Every thread a tale to spin,
Fearless hearts, where dreams begin.
Weaving love in colors bright,
Each story shared ignites the night.

In woven paths, our lives entwine,
Courage blooms, a sacred sign.
Through trials faced, we learn to dance,
In fearless threads, we take our chance.

A Journey of Unseen Bravery

Steps taken on an unseen road,
In whispered strength, we share our load.
Each day unfolds a quiet fight,
In hidden courage, we find our light.

With every breath, a new dawn breaks,
In silence held, a heart awakes.
Though unseen, our spirits soar,
In bravery's arms, we are much more.

Breaking Chains of Doubt

In shadows deep the fears reside,
Yet whispers soft must now abide.
With every step, the chains we break,
A path to light, a new awake.

The heart beats strong, the mind set free,
A mountain climbed, a distant sea.
With courage found and faith in hand,
We rise anew, we take a stand.

The doubts may fade like morning mist,
Each leap we take, a chance not missed.
Beyond the walls where silence lay,
A brighter dawn, our hearts display.

Together bound by dreams we choose,
In unity, we cannot lose.
For in the light of hope we shine,
Breaking chains, our spirits align.

The Call of Daring Dreams

A spark ignites, a journey starts,
With every hope, we share our hearts.
We chase the stars that light the night,
In daring dreams, we find our flight.

Through valleys deep and mountains high,
We hear the call, we will not shy.
With courage fierce and spirit bright,
We'll forge our path, embrace the light.

Each challenge faced, a tale untold,
With every step, we grow more bold.
In every heartbeat, passion flows,
In daring dreams, our purpose grows.

The winds of change, they guide our way,
In unity, we'll seize the day.
With every dream, we rise anew,
The call of daring dreams rings true.

A Whisper to the Wind

Beneath the stars, a secret shared,
In softest tones, our dreams are bared.
A whisper flows, the night a veil,
In stillness found, our spirits sail.

The rustling leaves, they hold our song,
Each note a promise, pure and strong.
We dance with shadows, light and grace,
In whispers soft, we find our place.

The world awakens as we roam,
In whispers sweet, we find our home.
With every breeze that sweeps the earth,
A gentle touch, a cherished birth.

So hear the call, let silence hear,
Our dreams released, we cast out fear.
With every whisper to the night,
A spark ignites, our hearts take flight.

Rising Above the Tempest

The skies grow dark, the winds do wail,
Yet in our hearts, we shall prevail.
With every storm, we find our might,
Rising above, we seek the light.

The waves may crash, the thunder roar,
Yet courage blooms upon the shore.
With steadfast souls, we stand as one,
Facing the tempest till it's done.

In trials fierce, our spirits soar,
Each challenge met, we long for more.
With hearts ablaze and eyes so bright,
Rising above, we chase the light.

For in the storm, we find our song,
In unity, we grow so strong.
Together bound, through night and day,
Rising above, we find our way.

Breaking Chains of Doubt

In shadows deep, my heart would dwell,
A whispering doubt, a silent spell.
But I gather strength, my spirit cries,
To break the chains, to rise and fly.

With every step, I find my voice,
Rejecting fear, embracing choice.
The chains that bind, they start to fray,
As I reclaim my brighter day.

I'll dance through storms, I'll face the night,
For in my heart, there burns a light.
The past may grip, but I'll break free,
With each bold move, I learn to be.

No longer lost, I chart my course,
With courage deep, a steady force.
The doubts may come, but now I see,
I hold the power, I set me free.

The Light Behind Closed Eyes

In quiet moments, dreams arise,
A canvas drawn beyond the skies.
With every heartbeat, colors swirl,
A world unknown begins to unfurl.

Behind closed eyes, I see my path,
A journey rich, beyond the wrath.
The light within, it starts to glow,
Illuminating all I know.

With whispered hopes, I chase the dawn,
As shadows fade, I move along.
Each secret wish, a gentle guide,
In stillness, I shall not hide.

The light behind, it calls to me,
In dreams, I find my destiny.
With every breath, I step anew,
Embracing all that I can do.

Climbing Higher than Yesterday

Step by step, I find my way,
With each new dawn, a brighter day.
The peaks may tempt, but I will rise,
Climbing higher to touch the skies.

With sweat and grit, I face my fears,
Transforming doubt into my cheers.
The summit calls, a distant view,
Each struggle fuels a strength anew.

And though I stumble, I shall stand,
In every fall, I learn and expand.
For as I climb, I find my pace,
With every push, I win the race.

The heights I seek, they stretch afar,
But I am bold, I am a star.
With every breath, I break away,
Climbing higher than yesterday.

In the Face of the Unknown

A road ahead, a path unseen,
With every choice, a chance to glean.
In the face of the unknown, I stand,
With open heart and steady hand.

The whispers call, they urge to dive,
Into the depths where dreams arrive.
I'll forge ahead, though fear may sing,
For in the dark, I'll find my wing.

With every step, I break the mold,
Unfolding stories yet untold.
The mystery dances, vibrant and free,
In the face of fear, there's strength in me.

So take my hand, let's face the night,
With courage rich, we'll find the light.
For in the unknown, we shall explore,
And find the magic, forevermore.

Dancing on the Edge of Fear

Beneath the moon's soft gaze, we sway,
Voices tremble, yet we stay.
With each heartbeat, we draw near,
Embracing life, despite the fear.

Footsteps light, like whispers shared,
In the shadows, we are bared.
Moments fleeting, yet so clear,
Together, we will persevere.

The dance of doubt begins to fade,
As courage wraps each step we've made.
With every twirl, we break the chain,
Reveling in the joy of pain.

So join me now, take my hand,
In this dance, we'll forever stand.
Through every storm, we'll find our way,
Embracing night, welcoming day.

A Heart's Whisper in the Storm

Amidst the thunder's fierce embrace,
A gentle whisper finds its place.
In every gust, my heart takes flight,
Guided by love, dispelling night.

The raindrops fall like fleeting tears,
Yet through the chaos, love endears.
In swirling winds, I hear the call,
A soothing voice that conquers all.

Each heartbeat pounds like distant drums,
With faith that steadfastly becomes.
When clouds grow dark and shadows loom,
Our hearts ignite, dispelling gloom.

So hold me close in this great storm,
With love as shelter, we stay warm.
Together strong, we shall not part,
In the tempest lies our heart.

Unmasking Shadows

In the silence, shadows creep,
Whispered secrets that we keep.
Veils around our hearts we find,
Unveiling truths we leave behind.

A flicker lights the darkened space,
Revealing fears we must embrace.
With fragile hands, we lift the mask,
To uncover what dare not bask.

Beneath the surface, wounds do ache,
But healing blooms with each mistake.
So step into the light, be bold,
And watch the shadows slowly fold.

Together, we will face the night,
As shadows yield to inner light.
For unmasking is a sacred art,
Transforming fears to a fresh start.

The Armor of Courage

In times of trial, stand your ground,
With courage strong, let hope abound.
A shield of faith, a sword of will,
Embrace the fight, the heart to thrill.

Through valleys deep and mountains high,
The armor shines, against the sky.
With every challenge, stronger still,
We rise anew, guided by thrill.

The echoes of despair may call,
Yet courage whispers, never fall.
Within your soul, a fire burns,
Embrace the scars, for strength returns.

With boots of valor, march on forth,
In darkness found, discover worth.
Together we shall bravely soar,
With hearts ablaze, we'll fear no more.

Echoes of the Untamed Spirit

In shadows deep, where whispers dwell,
The wild heart beats, a secret spell.
Through tangled woods, the courage flows,
Each path unmarked, where the spirit goes.

The moonlight dances on trembling leaves,
A symphony sung by the sighing breeze.
With every step, the past unwinds,
In echoes soft, the soul reminds.

To chase the dawn, to seek the night,
In every turn, there's pure delight.
Embrace the storm, let voices rise,
For in the wild, the spirit flies.

As mountains call, and rivers scream,
We wander free, lost in a dream.
A timeless quest, a joyous flight,
In echoes bright, we find our light.

Wings of Defiance

Beneath the clouds of doubt and fear,
There lies a voice, both bold and clear.
With wings outstretched, we claim the sky,
No chains can bind, no dream deny.

Through raging storms, we sail on high,
With each heartbeat, we dare to fly.
In realms unknown, we stake our claim,
With courage fierce, we stoke the flame.

The whispers dark may seek to bind,
But in our hearts, the fierce unwind.
With every leap, we break the mold,
Our spirits rise, forever bold.

So take a breath, the time is now,
To shed the doubt and make a vow.
With wings of defiance, we soar above,
A testament to strength and love.

Steps Beyond the Safety Net

A trembling heart on the edge of day,
The safety net feels far away.
With each small step, the courage grows,
Into the vast unknown, it goes.

The leap of faith, a daunting climb,
With whispers soft, we dare the sublime.
Through shadows cast, we find the light,
In every risk, a chance to ignite.

The path unfolds, a winding scene,
Embrace the wild, the unforeseen.
With every stumble, we rise anew,
In daring strides, our strength breaks through.

So cast aside the fear of fall,
For in each step, we hear the call.
Beyond the net, our spirits tread,
In steps of boldness, we forge ahead.

The Fire that Ignites the Heart

A spark within, a gentle glow,
The fire ignites, a fierce tableau.
In shadows cast by doubt's embrace,
The heart's true flame finds its place.

Through tempest winds and chilling nights,
Its warmth endures, our guiding light.
With every breath, it fans the flame,
A radiant dance, we will not tame.

In trials faced, the embers rise,
A conflagration in the skies.
Through passion's heat, we break apart,
To find the fire that ignites the heart.

So gather close, let spirits sing,
For in this blaze, the hope takes wing.
Together we'll burn, unafraid to start,
For life's great journey ignites the heart.

The Uncharted Map of MY Spirit

In the depths of my heart, a map unfolds,
Paths of dreams and stories untold.
With each step, I leave a trace,
Navigating this sacred space.

Stars above guide my way,
Amidst the shadows where I sway.
Ideas sprout like wildflowers,
Growing stronger by the hours.

Journeys beckon, call my name,
In this quest, I stake my claim.
Through valleys low and mountains high,
With brave resolve, I seek the sky.

The map is mine, a work of art,
Charting the uncharted in my heart.
With each twist and turn, I find my ground,
In the silence, my soul is found.

The Thorns of Uncertainty

In gardens where shadows loom near,
Thorns of doubt prick the veneer.
Yet beneath each painful steal,
Blooms of hope stagger to heal.

Wandering through the twilight haze,
Questions dance in a blurry maze.
Yet within the prickle and scrapes,
I find strength in my escape.

The fear that grips feels so real,
But courage whispers, I can heal.
With each thorn, I learn to grow,
Through the chaos, I'll surely flow.

Embracing the thorns on this path,
Transforming pain into a bath.
Where uncertainty reigns, I hold on tight,
For in the dark, I seek the light.

Flames of Unwavering Spirit

In the hearth of my being, a fire burns,
Flickering brightly, the world turns.
With every challenge, I stoke the flame,
Fueling passion, refusing to tame.

Through storms that rage and shadows that rise,
My spirit flickers, but never dies.
In the dance of embers, I find my way,
Carving hope through the night and day.

Against the winds of adversity's blow,
I stand firm, refusing to bow.
With flames igniting the dreams I chase,
Each spark, a beacon in this vast space.

The warmth of my heart lights the dark,
A testament held in each vibrant spark.
With unwavering spirit, I rise and soar,
In the flames of purpose, I am evermore.

The Edge of Possibility

At the precipice where dreams take flight,
I stand courageous, facing the height.
With wings of hope spread wide and free,
I leap into the vast mystery.

The horizon calls; the sky is bright,
In every heartbeat, a spark ignites.
Uncharted lands seem close at hand,
In this moment, I proudly stand.

The edge of fear meets the breath of change,
Where life spins wild and feels so strange.
With every whisper of the unknown,
I forge my path, courage my throne.

Dancing along this daring line,
I embrace the chaos, it's truly divine.
For in this leap, I find my grace,
At the edge of possibility, my sacred place.

The Fire of Resolve

In the depths of night, a spark ignites,
A promise whispered to the stars,
With every trial, our courage writes,
The story of dreams, no matter how far.

With ashes of doubt, we rise anew,
Burning bright with unwavering light,
Each step we take, a vow we pursue,
A dance of flames, fierce and bright.

Through storms that rage and winds that bite,
We stand as giants, bold and proud,
In the heart of struggle, we find our might,
Our resolve, a fire, unbowed.

And even when shadows threaten to claim,
The warmth within guides our way,
For the blaze of hope will always remain,
In the hearts of the brave, come what may.

Embracing the Unknown

With open arms, we greet the new,
Each dawn a canvas, fresh and clear,
Stepping into paths that few pursue,
Curiosity whispers, inviting us near.

Beyond the horizon, where dreams collide,
We shed the bounds of what we know,
In uncertainty's dance, we find our stride,
Like flowers blooming in the sun's glow.

Fear may linger, a shadow on the trail,
Yet freedom calls, a siren song,
In the heart of adventure, we shall prevail,
Boundless and wild, where we belong.

So take a leap, let your spirit soar,
Into the depths of the vast unknown,
For in every challenge, we find much more,
The joy of living, our truest tone.

Wings of a Fearless Heart

Beneath the weight of a thousand fears,
A heart beats strong, defying the night,
With every tear, a courage appears,
Unfolding wings, ready for flight.

In the face of doubt, we learn to rise,
Like eagles soaring on currents free,
With hopes unchained, we touch the skies,
A symphony played in bold harmony.

Through valleys deep and mountains high,
We chase the dream that calls our name,
For with each struggle, we learn to fly,
The fire within, an unquenched flame.

For in this journey, we find our song,
A melody of strength and grace,
With wings of a fearless heart, we belong,
Embracing life, we find our place.

The Strength of Silent Roars

In the quiet whispers, power resides,
A force unyielding, subtle yet strong,
With every heartbeat, resilience abides,
   Silence echoing where we belong.

Through battles fought in shadows, unseen,
We carry burdens that weigh like stone,
   Yet in our stillness, a spirit keen,
   Emerges boldly, never alone.

With eyes that search the depths of the soul,
   We rise above, refusing to break,
In the tempest's eye, we find our whole,
A quiet strength that none can shake.

And when the world grows weary and frail,
   We stand together, a unified roar,
A testament to trials that unveil,
The strength found in silence, forevermore.

Fragments of Fearless Dreams

In twilight's glow, the dreams ignite,
Scattered sparks in the endless night.
Shadows whisper of paths unseen,
Courage thrives where hope has been.

The heart beats strong, defying the gloom,
Each fragment rises, shattering doom.
Voices call from the edge of doubt,
In fearless flight, we stand and shout.

Mountains loom but we will climb,
Each step forward, a dance with time.
Fragments coalesce into a whole,
Fearless dreams, the anthem of the soul.

Together we weave a tapestry bright,
In every stitch, we find the light.
The shards of courage, bold and free,
In fearless dreams, we dare to be.

The Chronicle of Undaunted Souls

In pages worn, stories unfold,
Of souls undaunted, brave and bold.
Through trials faced, their spirits rise,
A chronicle written in endless skies.

With every tear and every laugh,
They carve their path on life's great graph.
United strength, their voices soar,
In courage found, they crave for more.

Through storms that rage and shadows cast,
They chase the dawn, forget the past.
Each heartbeat echoes, a tale unique,
An undaunted spirit, strong and sleek.

The chronicle flows, a timeless stream,
In every heartbeat, in every dream.
Their legacy shines like a guiding star,
In the hearts of many, they live on afar.

Harmonies of Defiance

In the silence, a melody brews,
Daring notes that refuse to lose.
With every chord, we break the chains,
Harmonies rise where courage reigns.

Voices blend in a fearless choir,
A song of hope that will inspire.
Each note a step against the tide,
In defiance, we stand, side by side.

Resonating through the darkest night,
Defiance shines, a beacon bright.
Unyielding rhythms, we will play,
For every heart that seeks a way.

Together we forge a vibrant sound,
In harmonies of strength, we're found.
With every song that breaks the norm,
We lift each other, brave and warm.

A Shield Made of Hope

In the shadows, a shield takes form,
Crafted from dreams, resilient and warm.
Each hope a layer, strong and bright,
Guarding the heart against the night.

When worries weigh, and fears align,
The shield of hope begins to shine.
Its strength is woven from joy and trust,
In every breath, a promise, a must.

With each challenge, we raise it high,
The battles fought, beneath the sky.
In moments dark, when spirits bend,
The shield of hope will never end.

Together we stand, united and vast,
With hope as our shield, we hold steadfast.
Through storms and trials, we will cope,
Armored by faith, we nurture hope.

Serendipity in the Storm

Raindrops dance on rooftops high,
A melody beneath the gray sky.
Lightning flickers, a flash of light,
Hope is born in the heart of night.

Chaos swirls like leaves in flight,
Yet within it, dreams take height.
In every downpour, joy can bloom,
Serendipity dispels the gloom.

A Symphony of Fearlessness

With hearts ablaze, we face the dark,
Each breath a note, each step a spark.
Fear once whispered, now sings aloud,
Together we rise, strong and proud.

The symphony swells, a bold embrace,
In unity, we find our place.
Marching forward, hand in hand,
Fearlessness weaves through every strand.

The Veil of Peaceful Courage

In silence, courage softly dwells,
Behind the veil, it gently swells.
With inner strength, we greet the dawn,
A quiet battle, but not withdrawn.

The heart is steady, the spirit free,
Facing the waves, like an anchored tree.
With every breath, courage we weave,
In shadows cast, we dare believe.

Beneath the Armor of Shadows

A cloak of night wraps 'round the soul,
Within the depths, we seek the whole.
Beneath the armor, light resides,
A flicker bold where shadow hides.

We journey through the night's embrace,
With strength unseen, we find our place.
In every echo, in every sigh,
Beneath the shadows, we learn to fly.

The Path of Unshed Tears

In shadows deep, they start to weave,
A silent trail where hearts grieve.
Each tear unshed, a story told,
In whispered depths, their sorrows unfold.

Like rivers lost, they find the night,
In memories of lost delight.
With every sigh, the echoes sound,
A path of pain beneath the ground.

Yet hope may bloom in darkest soil,
From grief's embrace, we rise, uncoil.
The skies may weep, yet stars shine bright,
For dawn will chase away the night.

So walk this path, though shadows call,
For through the tears, we learn to stand tall.
In every drop, a lesson pure,
The path of unshed tears will endure.

Unmasking the Lion Within

Beneath the surface, a roar confined,
A spirit brave, with strength aligned.
Unmask the fear, let courage soar,
Embrace the wild; let the heart explore.

In quiet moments, hear the call,
The lion stirs, to break the fall.
With every breath, the fire ignites,
To claim the day, to conquer nights.

The journey starts with a single stride,
In the embrace of the rising tide.
Face the mirror, the truth within,
And find the strength to begin again.

Unveil your heart, let the battle begin,
For every soul holds a lion's grin.
With each unmasking, dare to stand,
And take your place on this vast land.

Wings Unfurled

In the quiet dawn, wings start to rise,
A promise made beneath the skies.
With every heart, a dream unfolds,
A tale of courage, waiting, bold.

The winds will carry dreams untold,
Through valleys deep and mountains cold.
With every beat, the spirit soars,
Unlock the gates, and open doors.

With colors bright, like a sunrise glow,
They dance and twirl, in the flow.
Embracing freedom, the sky their friend,
With wings unfurled, the dreams ascend.

So take the leap, let your heart steer,
For in the flight, there's nothing to fear.
The world awaits, with arms outspread,
In every journey, let love be bred.

The Sound of Heartbeats in Courage

In the silence, a rhythm thrums,
The heartbeat whispers, courage comes.
With every pulse, a tale awakes,
In the quiet strength, the spirit breaks.

Across the dark, the echoes call,
In unity, we rise, we fall.
Through every fight, the hearts align,
A symphony of souls, divine.

Each breath a promise, each thump a vow,
In the face of fear, we stand and bow.
For in our chest, a fire ignites,
The sound of heartbeats, brave in nights.

So listen close, to the world around,
In the heartbeat's rush, hope is found.
Together, we surge, like waves in the sea,
The sound of courage setting us free.

Boundless Horizons Await

The sun kisses the dawn, so bright,
Birds take flight in sheer delight,
Waves whisper secrets to the shore,
Endless paths we long to explore.

Mountains rise with regal grace,
Clouds drift lightly, dreams embrace,
Each step forward, hearts ignite,
Boundless horizons, pure and white.

Fields of gold and skies of blue,
Possibilities come into view,
With every breath, we break the chain,
In freedom's song, we dance again.

Hope unfurls like petals bright,
Guiding souls through day and night,
Together we chase what is fated,
For boundless horizons await, created.

Navigating the Depths

Beneath the surface, shadows sway,
In silent depths, fears often play,
Waves crash hard against the soul,
Guiding journeys to become whole.

With stars as maps, we chart our way,
Through darkened waters, night and day,
Each heartbeat sound, a guiding light,
Navigating through the deepest night.

Tides may pull with whispered doubt,
Yet courage rises, fierce and stout,
In stormy seas, we hold our own,
Finding strength we never have known.

And when the calm returns again,
We stand as one, embracing gain,
For through the depths, we've always grown,
Navigating storms, we're not alone.

Shattered Shields and New Armor

Once I wore a shield so strong,
But cracks appeared where I belonged,
Shattered dreams beneath the weight,
Yet from the ruins, I create.

New armor forged in flames of pain,
Each scar a tale, not born in vain,
With every piece, I rise anew,
Resilience blooms, fierce and true.

The past may haunt with bitter sighs,
But strength is found in battle cries,
From shattered shields, my spirit soars,
Embracing life with open doors.

Each step I take, a warrior's grace,
In knowing well my rightful place,
For I am more than broken parts,
Shattered shields and new armor in my heart.

Voices of the Unafraid

Whispers echo through the night,
Voices rise, igniting light,
Together strong, we stand and fight,
The unafraid, our hearts take flight.

Against the tide of doubt and fear,
Courage sings, loud and clear,
With every word, we weave our fate,
United in strength, resists the hate.

In the shadows, hope takes form,
We break the chains; we shift the norm,
Each voice a spark, together brave,
In numbers we find the strength to save.

So let us rise, unbowed, unchained,
In our hearts, love is uncontained,
For in the chorus, truth is laid,
We are the voices of the unafraid.

The Dawning of Audacity

In shadows deep, dreams start to rise,
A flicker of hope, beneath the skies.
With brave hearts beating, we take our stand,
Chasing the light across the land.

Each step a whisper, shaking the ground,
Words like thunder, in silence found.
We reach for the stars, unchained, unbowed,
The dawn breaks bright, we shout it loud.

Voices unite, a tapestry spun,
Together we shine, like gold in the sun.
Embracing the fierce, the fire within,
In this new dawn, let courage begin.

So here we stand, with hearts set free,
The audacity flows, an endless sea.
With dreams in our hands, we dare to believe,
In the dawning light, we shall achieve.

Serenade of the Bold

By moonlit nights, the brave take flight,
A serenade sung, chasing the night.
With every chord, our spirits rise,
Reaching for stars, in velvet skies.

In courage's name, we dance and sway,
Each heartbeat echoes, come what may.
Fear melts away with each gentle strum,
In this song of life, we overcome.

Voices entwined, a powerful throng,
Together in harmony, we sing our song.
The world may tremble, but we stand tall,
In the serenade of the bold, we call.

So raise your voice, let the anthem soar,
With belief unyielding, we seek for more.
In unity found, we rise and unfold,
The magic persists, in tales retold.

Crossing Thresholds

At the door's edge, we pause and breathe,
Life's mysteries beckon, if we believe.
With trembling hands, we push the wood,
Venturing forth into the good.

Each threshold crossed, a tale we weave,
Moments of doubt, that we perceive.
But courage whispers, softly it calls,
Together we conquer, together we fall.

Through valleys deep, and mountains high,
With every step, we aim for the sky.
Boundless the journey, our spirits sing,
For in crossing boundaries, we discover spring.

So tread with purpose, let passion guide,
Embrace the unknown, with arms open wide.
In every horizon, new paths await,
In crossing thresholds, we shape our fate.

Voicing the Silent Heart

In quiet corners, whispers reside,
Silent feelings that we often hide.
But deep inside, a fire glows bright,
Yearning to speak, to share the light.

With trembling voices, we dare to begin,
To voice the stories buried within.
A tapestry woven from hope and pain,
In this sacred space, we break the chain.

For every heartbeat, a lesson learned,
Through tears and laughter, the heart has burned.
In unity found, our spirits align,
To voice the silent, let our truths shine.

So speak with courage, let the echoes flow,
For every heart has its story to show.
Together we rise, in love's warm embrace,
Voicing the silent, we find our place.

Beyond the Walls of Worry

In shadows deep where doubts reside,
We seek to find a brighter guide.
With every breath, we break the chain,
And dance beneath the falling rain.

The whispers fade, the courage grows,
A path emerges, life bestows.
Each step a choice, a drumbeat bold,
In harmony, our dreams unfold.

Together we will rise and soar,
United hearts, we become more.
Beyond the walls, the light breaks free,
A tapestry of possibility.

So cast aside your fears tonight,
And let your spirit take to flight.
For in the realm where hope is sown,
We'll build a world we've never known.

Dreaming Out Loud

In twilight's hush, the visions spark,
A symphony in every heart.
From silent thoughts to words we share,
We lift the veil with tender care.

With eyes aglow, we dare to dream,
And chase the sun's enchanting beam.
Reality bends to will and fire,
In the echo of our soul's desire.

As whispers turn to heartfelt cries,
The universe aligns the skies.
We weave our hopes in bright array,
And paint the night in shades of play.

So raise your voice, let echoes ring,
In every note, our spirits sing.
Dreaming out loud, we'll find our way,
A journey born from night to day.

An Odyssey Beyond Comfort

Beneath the stars, the paths unfold,
To realms of stories yet untold.
With trembling hearts, we venture far,
Embracing change, our guiding star.

In every step, the world expands,
Through uncharted seas and distant lands.
With courage found in venture's call,
We rise and stumble, yet stand tall.

The fires burn within our cores,
As we unlock those ancient doors.
In unfamiliar, we find our spark,
Transforming darkness into art.

This odyssey, though fraught with fears,
Will yield the strength of countless years.
Beyond comfort's grasp, we learn to roam,
Creating worlds, we call our home.

The Language of Fearless Hearts

In silent realms where bravest tread,
The language formed, the words unsaid.
With fearless hearts, we break the mold,
A tapestry of truths retold.

Through passion's fire, we learn to speak,
Beneath the scars, the spirit's peak.
For every glance, a universe,
In connection, we find our verse.

With open hands, and minds embraced,
We gather strength in every space.
This language flows, a river wide,
We bridge the gap, no need to hide.

So let us vow to share our song,
In fearless hearts, together strong.
For love's pure voice is what we crave,
A melody that frees, saves.